Small Business Starters Guide

The Ultimate Guide to Starting a Small Business

By Gardner P. Saint

Table of Contents

Introduction:
Why Create a Business?

Wouldn't it be nice to be your own boss? You don't have to start work on hours you don't want to, you never have to worry about your boss taking back that day he or she promised you off, and you can associate yourself with people you can trust and work well with. Too bad it's a pipe dream, right?

Wrong! Starting your own business is something that's not just limited to people who have money to burn. Anyone can start a business, and with the Internet so readily available, it's easier than ever. You can practically run a business in the comfort of your own apartment, and you don't even have to be face-to-face with anyone if you're not a people person.

In this book, we'll be tackling two types of business: brick and mortar and ecommerce. What do those terms mean? Let's break it down for you.

Brick and Mortar

Simply put, brick and mortar just means a traditional, offline business. The store you go to whenever you get your groceries is brick and mortar. That little coffee shop you visit on occasion is brick and mortar. That office you go to in order to file taxes is brick and mortar. That's all it means.

Of course, with the rising popularity of online shopping, brick and mortar has some stiff competition. But we'll get to that later on in the book.

Ecommerce

Ecommerce is a business where goods, services, and transactions are all done through the Internet. Amazon.com and Ebay.com come to mind when you think of online stores, but anything conducted online is considered ecommerce. That digital artist selling commissions is ecommerce, for instance. Once seen as a novelty, more and more are relying on online shopping to do their business. For those who are poor, online is seen as a good way to start. We'll discuss that later in the book.

More Reasons Why You Should Start Your Own Business

Besides being your own boss, why else should you start your own business? Here are a few reasons to do so.

Tax Breaks!

There are two guarantees in life: death and taxes. Being an employee working at a 9-5, it's frustrating seeing some of your paycheck going to Uncle Sam, and it's more annoying trying to get some of that money back come tax season.

With running your own business, however, you can get some good write-offs. Run a business in your own home? The rent, electricity, Internet service, cell phone bill, and anything relevant to the job can be a write-off. If you have to drive to meet clients, and pay money for shipping, that can be a write-off. If the business is done with your spouse or other family members, there are opportunities for breaks as well. That service fee you use for transactions? A write-off! The possibilities go on and on.

Of course, we're not tax professionals. Always consult a professional whenever you do your taxes.

Lots of Job Security

Worried about being laid off? You can't be laid off if you're in control. Worried about saying something wrong on Facebook, and your boss, who forced you to be friends, fires you because he or she didn't like what you had to say? Don't have to worry about that. In an age where people get fired for the dumbest reason, you don't have to be one of those.

A Chance to Learn Something and be an Expert

It's hard to grow as a person doing the same boring tasks at your workplace. By owning a business, however, you can learn valuable skills. From taking risks to changing your strategy depending on trends, you'll practically learn something new every day.

A Chance to Be Inspired

By being a business owner, you'll be associating yourself with other business owners as well. From CEOs of large companies to owners of a mom and pop shop, you'll learn tips, make friends, and work together to improve the world around you. You won't just be talking to your co-worker about who won the basketball game last night.

Disadvantages

Of course, there are disadvantages as well, from financial risk to working 24/7 during your initial startup. Every way of making a living has its pros and cons, and starting your business is as well.

However, we'll make sure you can minimize the risks so you'll have the determination to start your own business. Let's begin.

Chapter 1:
Researching Your Business

Sometimes in life, it's worth it to rush into things blindly. Other times, you shouldn't jump the gun. Starting your business is definitely the latter. You'll be spending a good chunk of your time doing research, and this doesn't mean Googling a few things and you're done.

You'll also be doing research on yourself, too. What do we mean by this?

What Can You Turn Into a Business?

Society gives you mixed signals when it comes to doing something you like. Some say your work should be something you enjoy doing, while others say you should go for the job that gives you the most money, regardless if it's your thing or not.

Well, for your business, you definitely need to base it on something you enjoy doing. Is your passion cooking? Start a restaurant! Starving artist? Sell your art! Good with numbers? Start an accounting firm! The list goes on. If you base your business on something you enjoy doing, you'll have a higher chance of succeeding. So look at your muses and see if anything is profitable.

Profitable is the Key

Of course, not all passions make for a good business. If your passion is skiing, it still wouldn't be a good idea to sell skiing equipment in a place that hardly gets snow. You'll still need to look at what's profitable in your area, and if you're doing online shopping, it gets even messier. We'll look at brick and mortar vs. ecommerce in their own individual chapters.

Know Your Audience

When planning your business, get a general idea of who your audience will primarily consist of. Are you starting a video game store? Then a chunk of your audience is probably teens and young adults, with a few veteran gamers here and there. Along with some parents who are buying games for their children.

If you're starting a diner in the boonies, expect a variety of older people, from middle-aged blue collar workers to the gossiping elderly.

But it'll be more than just stereotyping your audience. You need to get in their heads. Who are they? What are their desires? Do they want to buy your product? What's their typical income? What do they desire in customer service? What parts of town do they frequent? What websites do they visit?

To figure that out, you'll have to be looking up some data. Figuring out your potential audience's age, sex, income, education, etc., can be obtained through the Census, and through available public records.

You need more than raw data, though! You also need to figure out your customers' beliefs and lifestyles. To do that, look up interviews and surveys. If your business caters to Millennials, there are tons of articles telling you how most of them believe, and what they want in a business.

What's the Competition?

You'll more than likely have competition. Whether it's other businesses established before yours, or players in the future, you need to know your enemy. Your competition strategy will all depend on what type of business you have and where you are.

If you live in a small town, you may have little to no competition, and it'll be easier seeing how your competitors run your business. If you live in the city, you may have lots of competition, and thus more to research.

Online, it gets even murkier. You may have limitless competition, and you'll always be on your toes. We'll discuss that more in its respective chapter, though.

Know Your Finances!

As you should know, a business requires you to spend money before you can make any. That may sound contradictory, but it's how the game works. How much money you need depends on what you're doing. Obviously, selling your art online will require you to spend little. You don't need a building to do that; everything in your home will suffice. You may need some paper, an easel, some supplies, and whatnot, but it isn't going to break your bank.

But if you're starting a brick and mortar, you may have to think about the cost of rent, the legal fees, how much you'll be paying your employees, the security deposit, insurance, the upkeep... it takes a lot, and if you go into it unplanned, you may end up shooting yourself in the foot.

So with that all said, let's look at brick and mortar.

Chapter 2:
Starting Up a Brick and Mortar

If you've done your planning, you've probably calculated how much it will be to rent your potential business. Or maybe you're building it from scratch?

We can't tell you how much it's going to cost to start up your brick and mortar. It all depends on your location, what you're selling, and other circumstances. As usual, consult a finance professional to calculate how much it's going to cost. Doing all the math works as well, but if you're new to the business, you may overlook a few costs.

Some Important Things to Know

Know Your Laws

Unless you're in the black market, you need to be on the good side of the law whenever you're starting your business, and these laws will be local, state, and federal. Read up on your state and town's laws before you build. Here are some things you'll generally be facing, however.

A Tax ID

Here's that T-word again. To operate a business, you'll need to have a tax ID handy. Also known as an Employer Identification number, or EIN. You can typically apply for one online through the IRS's website. Make sure you have one before starting your business. You'll be identified as a business this way.

Permits

Your business will need to have permits in order to run. As we said, this will all depend on where you live, so there's no one size fits all answer to this. Some permits you may need to run into include a fire department permit, a health department permit, a certificate of occupancy, a building construction permit, and more. Look into your laws as you plan your business.

Employee Regulations

If you'll be hiring employees, make sure you look into the employment laws as well. There will be different laws, such as how long minors can work and how many breaks are required.

You shouldn't need a law to tell you that you should probably treat your employees well, though. Don't be that boss everyone hates.

Competition

Once you start up your business, you may be wondering how you can stifle the competition. That's the thing. You need to learn who's you're up against.

Depending on where you live, this will be easy, hard or nonexistent. For instance, if you're the only business of your kind in a small town, you have no competition (although, if there are businesses similar to yours in another town, check them out.) If you're in a big city, you may have a lot more competition than you think. There may be online competition as well, but we'll talk about that later.

Here are some tips to know your enemy:

- Perhaps the most obvious one, you should learn your competitor's price. Are they selling it for cheaper? See if it's possible to lower your prices to match theirs. Are the prices more expensive? You could raise your prices to make it a little under theirs.
- Visit the place and look at the building. What makes the building pop to a customer? Are there decorations? A flashy sign? How does it look indoors?
- Be a customer. See how the shelves are organized, and figure out how easy it is to buy a product there. Go through the line to see how fast the employers are. Try contacting their customer service and see how it works.
- Where are they located? If you haven't started up your business yet, consider putting it near the area they are, if the business is attracting plenty of customers.

In simpler terms, it all boils down to figuring out what the competition does, and planning a way to do what they do, only better.

Brick and Mortar Vs. Online

The rise of online shopping has some saying that brick and mortar stores are doomed. With the ability to buy anything as easy as reaching into your pocket and shopping with your smartphone, there's a reason why online shopping is on the rise. Here are a few reasons some are preferring online shopping to brick and mortar.

Convenience

Dress up, get out of the house, drive to the store, wait in line, check out, drive back. None of that applies when shopping online. And if you're not a people person, even better! No need to talk to a cashier, or deal with an awkward conversation with another shopper.

Open 24/7

Most brick and mortars aren't run 24/7. And most small businesses have to deal with ordinary, 9-5 hours. For some customers, these hours aren't convenient. If a customer stays up until six in the morning, they may do their shopping on the Internet.

It Tends to Be Cheaper

There was a time when online shopping didn't seem to be worth it. The cost of shipping tended to make the product cost as much as it would in the store, and no one likes to wait a week to get a product.

Those days are ending. With free shipment plans, options for two day (and sometimes in a few hours) shipping, and the lack of a middleman making the prices cheaper than stores, it's no wonder some choose online.

In fact, some customers will be showroomers. Showrooming is when a customer walks into a store, sees a product they're interested in, and then uses their smartphone to look at the prices online. If they find the product for cheaper on the Internet, they'll order it online instead of buying it from the store.

As a brick and mortar business owner, you may despise these people, but they are just looking for the best deal. You'll need to think of different ways to combat the online competition.

Don't Combat the Internet. Work in Harmony With it!

The Internet isn't going anywhere, and fighting it is an uphill battle. Not allowing phones will make you seem insane, and ignoring ecommerce altogether is a bad move. Many will still shop in brick and mortar, after all. For some, they like being in a place where they can know what they're buying, and ask any questions if they need to. So physical shops still have use, and here are some ways you can work in harmony with the World Wide Web.

Why Not Both?

Use the Internet as an extension of your business. Can you show your inventory online, and potentially ship it to any online shoppers? If you have a restaurant, can you cater?

Even if you can't deliver online, you can still use the Internet to make the shopping experience easier for your customers. For instance, giving your customers the option of online reservation (there's an app for that, too,) can make them skip the lines and skip the wait. This is especially important if your business is for younger people.

How to Hire

We'll close off this chapter by giving you a few tips on how to hire great employees to run your business. The process sounds simple, but hiring is an art, as you'll soon find out.

Hire the Most Qualified

This may sound obvious, but many small business owners, especially in small towns, tend to hire someone they know. This is called cronyism, and even though everyone does it, it's still frowned upon. When deciding who you should hire, be objective and don't let your biases seep through.

Look for Experience, but Give Newbies a Chance as Well

If your business is low-skill labor, like fast food, don't just hire people with experience. Allow a newbie to prove his or her mettle. Who knows? They may impress you.

Be Clear About the Job Description

Detail what the job is going to entail, and stick with it. Don't make a fry cook clean up the restaurant without telling them beforehand. Don't say you have flexible hours when you don't. Being deceived can lower employee morale, which is something you don't want.

Never Stop Looking

Even if you think your business doesn't need more, always accept applications. You never know when someone's going to quit out of the blue. No one likes an understaffed business, so don't allow yours to be.

Spread the Word

Don't just put a 'Now hiring' sign on the door. Post in newspapers, on web forums, and around town that you're looking for someone. This way, you get the best pool of potential employees possible.

Chapter 3:
Starting Up an Online Business

So Much Easier!

Anyone can start their own business online. Whether you're a broke college kid or living in a mansion, the Internet has become so available and so easy for anyone to start up their own business, you'll be selling stuff in no time. But where should you sell at?

Selling on an Ecommerce Site Vs. Your Own

Amazon, eBay, Etsy, and so many other online shops have made it easier than ever to start your own business. Just create an account, enter information relevant to you, and you're pretty much set on starting your own business.

But what about creating your own website and your own store? Should you do that instead of sell on already established websites? There are pros and cons to doing both, and here are just a few:

Selling on Another Site

Pros

Easy to Set Up

As we said, it's easy to create an account and start selling. You don't need to worry about building your own perfect website, or getting traffic into the site in general.

It's Trusted

Not everyone feels comfortable giving out their payment information to a mom and pop website. That sounds silly, but you have to admit, it's different to give a site your information than to swipe your card at a shop. Amazon, eBay, Etsy, and all the other sites are household names.

It's not only card information people are worried about, though. Some like peace of mind when buying a protect, and they like to have a neutral third party, in this case, the site, handling things should there be a dispute.

Easy to See the Competition

Odds are, the product you're selling will be similar to something else. So all you need to do is to look at your competitor's product, look at the price, read the reviews, and you'll have a good idea on how to compete.

Cons

Those Service Fees

Service fees are understandable. Amazon, eBay, etc., have to make money somehow, and to do that, they take a bit off your profit. It's usually not that much, around 10% or so, but it can really add up after a while.

You're Under Their Thumb

Marketplace sites have rules on what you can sell. Again, like the service fees, there are reasons this exist, and they're a necessary evil. Before you sell, you should definitely read the site's rules, and if they don't gel with you, find another site.

Even so, the rules can change any time. What's okay one day may be forbidden the next. Plus, the site can terminate your account any time? Dispute gone sour? Payment information messed up? Be aware at all times.

Limited Payment Options

Some market sites want you to only use a card. Some want you to only use PayPal. And some want you to only use another odd method of payment. This shouldn't be an issue for most people, but you always get that one customer who may not like using PayPal, or doesn't own a card.

And this one can be both a pro and a con:

Customer Feedback

Most marketplace sites give the customers an option to rate and review your product. On one hand, if your product is getting rave reviews, it'll get noticed right away. Plus, feedback is good. It allows you constructive criticism on your product, allowing you to learn as you go.

However, if your product is getting negative reviews, it may put a damper on your sales.

Now, you may say, "Well, you shouldn't be selling a bad product if you don't want bad reviews." That may be true. However, people can give you negative reviews because of things that are irrelevant to the product or their own fault. The customer didn't follow the instructions on your product, and is blaming the product for it. The mail messed up the product, yet you're getting the blame. Or, it could be a book or other piece of art that's well-written, but the first person who happened to review it just didn't care for it.

All it takes is one negative review to turn customers away from your product. That's why some sellers, as unethical as this practice seems, pay people to leave positive reviews on their product.

Starting Your Own Site

Pros

Your Site, Your Rules

You can sell whatever you want as long as it's legal, you can set up your own payment methods, don't have to worry about a third party settling your dispute, and you can enable or disable reviews. And with your website, you can design it however you like to appeal to the product's theme, as well as your personality.

No Service Fees

This one is self-explanatory. You get to keep more of your money. What's not to like!

Teaches You Valuable Skills

You'll have to market your product a lot more than you would on a marketplace site. You'll learn about SEO, what type of website customers like, what payment plans are preferred, and the list goes on and on.

Cons

It's Costlier

You have everything you need if you sell on Amazon or eBay. However, you'll usually have to build your own website from scratch, and it'll probably take some trial and error figuring out what customers want. Unless you can do it yourself, you'll be paying someone to build your site, maintain your ad campaign, and the list goes on.

Riskier

With higher cost comes a higher risk. If your site fails, you'll be wasting a lot of money. Perhaps you should make your own site whenever you get a following. Which leads us to our next recommendation...

Do Both!

Perhaps you should start selling on a marketplace website, and then, when you obtain enough of a following and have a higher budget, you make your own website. You can even continue selling stuff on the marketplace site. It's the Internet; you can set up as many shops as you want.

Chapter 4:
Advertising and Marketing

No one likes being advertised to, but let's face it, most people go to a business because they saw it on a TV, saw a sign for it, or heard it through friends. To get the word out, you should have a good advertising campaign going, and it should fit into your budget.

You're probably not ready to put your business on TV just yet, but here are some ways you can get your local business out there. Even if you have a brick and mortar business, some of these strategies are online, because, let's face it, online advertising is the future. It's cheap, and it gets the point across. We'll start with brick and mortar advertising.

Bulletin Boards

Odds are, different areas in your town have bulletin boards, whether it's public or tucked away In another business. Bulletin boards allow you to pin an ad for your business and let customers of another place see it. People, especially those who have recently moved to a town, love searching bulletin boards to see what is happening in their town.

Of course, some bulletin boards have different advertising rules, so don't post your advertisement before talking with whoever runs the place you're in.

Flyers

Coming out of a grocery store and seeing that someone plastered a flyer on your car can be annoying, but it does get eyes noticing. Try printing out some fliers, go to a retailer, and put them on any cars you can see. Alternatively, you can go to apartment complexes and do the same thing to people's doors.

Before you do that, look at the property you're advertising on's rules. Some places don't care if there are solicitors, and some do.

Shirts!

People love looking at each other's shirts. Whenever finding a potential friend or even lover, a shirt can tell you a lot about a person. A good way to advertise is to sell shirts to your customers, or wear one of your own, giving information about the company you run.

Automobile Advertising

Another thing people are looking at is what's on your car. You can sell bumper stickers, or put some on your car, that tell others about your business. If you don't want to do that, you can always write on your car. It's quite easy to do, and it's effective. Especially if the town you live in primarily relies on personal vehicles as transportation

Your Own Booth

Next time there's a relevant convention, or even something such as a flea market, why not rent your own booth? You'll meet many potential customers, all looking to try everything, and it will allow you to show them samples of what you're selling.

Door Hangers

You can make your own door hangers, advertising your business, and hang them on people's doors. Some will appreciate getting advertised to, and will check out your business. Always make sure to know the rules before you solicit, though!

A Publicity Stunt

Sometimes, you have to think outside the box to get everyone's attention. You may not be able to set a world record, but you can get some stares. For example, if you know someone who can do some skateboarding tricks, have them skate off the steepest rail in the town, and use it as a way to advertise.

Local Media

Does your town have a newspaper? Radio station? Local television station? Depending on how small your town is, it may be affordable to advertise on it. Look into the different media outlets and see if you can afford an advertisement. This is especially important if your audience is consisted of older people, who may use older forms of media.

Recommendation

The best way to get new customers is from your existing words. Encourage your customers to get the word out about your business. If a customer recommends your business to someone, you can even give that customer rewards, such as discounts, if the new customer tells you the old customer sent them.

Now, here are some online ways to advertise. Many of these will work, and are, in fact, vital, for your brick and mortar as well.

Social Media

No matter if your business is offline or online, having a social media campaign is a good way to get your business out there. Have a Facebook page. Make an Instagram. Start up a Twitter. On Facebook, you can even pay for ads.

Being on social media, you can talk to other users as well. As we said, people don't like being advertised to, so you have to be a little sneaky about it. For example, if you run a restaurant that serves burgers, look up local hashtags about burgers, and comment things like, "Looks tasty." The users will see your handle, be curious about your business, and check it out.

Sharing is Caring

When running a social media campaign, one of the goals is to get as many people to share your content as possible. Some ways to do this include:

A Simple Reminder

Telling your audience to like and share after every post can surprisingly be effective. Especially if you give them a reason to like and share. Which brings us to our next point...

Hold Contests

Everyone loves free stuff. Make a giveaway, with the rules being whoever likes and shares the post enters. Offer them a sample of your product, or maybe give them a discount. Whatever you do, it'll get more to look at your product, and thus increase your audience.

Sometimes, Irrelevancy Works Too

It doesn't always have to be about your business. Posting a relatable meme will get a lot of attention to your page. Taking advantage of the latest trends works as well. Of course, do this in moderation. Don't turn your Facebook page into another generic meme page, where your audience ignores what you're selling altogether.

Promote on Forums

Message boards, Facebook groups, and chat rooms are all grounds for you to advertise your product. Just make sure advertising is okay with the group. Usually, you can talk to an admin before promoting.

Of course, the worse that'll happen to you if you advertise on a forum is that you get banned from said forum. However, it's always good to ask before you post.

Have Good SEO

One of the ways to get your side noticed is through SEO, or Search Engine Optimization. A site with good SEO will appear on the front page of Google or another search engine when someone uses particular keywords. For example, if your website has the words, "Tasty hamburgers" all over it, someone typing "tasty hamburgers" may find your business.

It's more complicated than it sounds, and you'll more than likely need an SEO expert to optimize your site. We could write a book on this alone.

Try a PPC Campaign

PPC, or Pay Per Click, is when you set up an ad for your site, which will appear in the search results of Google, and you pay the host whenever someone clicks on the advertisement. It's another effective way to advertise, and like PPC, may require you to consult an expert in order to run an effective ad.

Customer Retention

If you think you should focus your marketing campaign solely on getting new customers, you're fighting only half the battle. You don't want a customer to be one time only; you want a customer who will keep frequenting your business. That's where customer retention comes in.

Newsletters

Ask every customer if they want to sign up for a newsletter. Newsletters contain, well, news about your business. Upcoming deals, new merchandise, coupons, and improvements to the shop are just a few things you can announce in your newsletter.

Newsletters can be done through email or snail mail. You may think that email is the way to go, as it's cheaper, but snail mail is useful too. First, snail mail feels a lot more personal than getting an email. Not only that, but there's a chance a spam filter could prevent your customers from seeing the email.

Avoid a High Bounce Rate

A bounce rate is when a customer lands on your website's landing page (be it the main page or a page taken to them via an ad,) and leaves the site before making a purchase (or doing something else you want them to do). There are many reasons a customer may bounce, and you're not going to sell everyone who lands on your page. Here are a few ways you can lower that bounce rate, however.

Speed Up Your Site

There was a time when slow websites were the norm. That has long changed. If your site isn't ready to view within a few seconds after a visitor clicks on it, they may back away. Everyone on the Net is impatient, after all.

Consult an expert and see what's preventing your site from loading fast enough. Sometimes, the change can be simple, and other times, it may require a renovation.

Don't Forget About Mobile!

If you haven't created a website that's friendly to mobile users, you're doing it all wrong. With so many using their phones to surf a web, creating a site only designed for desktop will cause a high bounce rate. So make a mobile-friendly version of your site at all costs.

Make the Site Simple

Does your customer have to jump through hoops to get what they want? Do they have to go through page upon page to find their product? A complex website is good in some cases, but for marketing purposes, keep it as simple as possible. Look at a few websites you shop at. What do you like about the site's design? What could be improved? Write these comments down and use them to improve your own website.

Chapter 5:
Run a Business With a Peace of Mind

We'll end this book by giving you a few tips to reduce risk when running a business. As we said before, running a business does require some risk, but there are ways to make sure you don't go totally bankrupt, or get caught with your pants down, in the process.

Buy Insurance

You never know how important insurance can be until an incident happens that could have been prevented with it. Having homeowner's insurance is one thing, but also look into liability insurance as well. If your area is prone to storms, get insurance that fits. Of course, you don't want to go too insurance crazy and get volcano insurance, but weigh your options nonetheless.

Prevent Problems from Happening in the First Place

If you have a little money to spend, why not install some sprinklers? You never know when a fire may happen. Or, maybe you could install some security cameras. It can make the difference between recovering stolen property and having property lost to time. Insurance can help, but preventing the problem in the first place will save you a lot of headaches.

Liability

No one likes to be slapped with an insane lawsuit, nor be in trouble if the product is defective. Look into liability insurance and see what it covers. Another thing is to minimize risk in your business to avoid any injuries. Having clear warranty and return policies is another good idea, as well as maximizing customer service. Keep all the customers happy, and you'll be less at risk.

If All Else Fails, Cash Out

The writing is on the wall. Your business is failing. Maybe there's a new business that you can't compete with, or everyone's just not interested in what you're selling.

Sometimes, businesses may have dry spells they have to sift through in order to grow. But if nothing's working, and it appears as though your business is going downhill, don't be afraid to cash out. Sell your business, take your assets, and have a happy retirement. Or create a new business. Sometimes, a fresh start is what you need.

Conclusion

Now you know the basics on how to start and run a business, online and offline. Of course, this isn't the ultimate Bible or anything; just a way for newcomers, as well as those curious about starting a business, to see what may be on the horizon.

If you're thinking of starting your own business, follow what we say and do more research. Don't just take our word for it; research all you can about starting a business. It's better not to rush things than it is to jump in when the water is still shallow.

Anyway, if you enjoyed this book, please give it a review on its proper page. If you've been paying attention, you know a good review is essential for a business, so we encourage you do so. Whether you want to praise this book or give it criticism is up to you. Just know that your feedback is important, and we'll use your comments to improve future works.

www.ingramcontent.com/pod-product-compliance
Lightning Source LLC
Chambersburg PA
CBHW070341190526
45169CB00005B/1996